GOLF AFTER FORTY

Golf After Forty

By H. A. HATTSTROM

Photographic Illustrations by
W. B. BAXTER

HALL PUBLISHING COMPANY

I DEDICATE THIS BOOK to my son,
Dr. John Allan Hattstrom
of the United States Army Air Forces.

Contents

THE THEORY OF THE FLATFOOT MANNER . . . 13

THE GRIP 21

THE STANCE 27

THE WOODS 37

THE IRONS 59

THE SHORT GAME 73

    THE CUT SHOT 80
    THE CHIP SHOT 88
    THE RUN-UP SHOT 94

THE TRAP SHOT 99

THE HATTSTROM "IN-LINE"
PUTTING TECHNIQUE 107

    THE PUTTING GRIP 113
    THE PUTTING STANCE 118
    THE PENDULUM STROKE 123
    SOME PUTTING SUGGESTIONS 128

A FEW DON'TS 131

FOR THE ADVANCED GOLFER 147

Illustrations

1. Left Hand Grip — 24
2. The Vardon Over-lapping Grip — 25
3. The Two-Handed Grip — 26
4. Square Stance — 30
5. Side View of Square Stance — 31
6. Closed Stance — 32
7. Side View of Closed Stance — 33
8. Open Stance — 34
9. Side View of Open Stance — 35
10. The Drive Address — 42
11. The Drag Back — 43
12. The Upswing — 44
13. Top of Back Swing — 45
14. Top of Back Swing, Side View — 46
15. Half Way Down — 47
16. Half Way Down, Side View — 48
17. Three Quarters Down — 49
18. Impact — 50
19. Impact, Side View — 51
20. The Follow Through — 52
21. Finish of Swing — 53
22. 1 to 7 O'Clock Position — 54
23. 1 to 7 O'Clock Position, Side View — 55
24. 12 to 6 O'Clock Position — 56
25. 11 to 5 O'Clock Position — 57
26. Mid-Iron Stance — 64
27. Niblick Stance — 65
28. Stance and Address for No. 5 Iron — 66
29. Side View of No. 5 Iron Stance and Address — 67
30. Top of Iron Swing — 68
31. Top of Iron Swing, Side View — 69
32. Half Way Down — 70
33. Instant Before Impact — 71
34. Taking of Divot — 72
35. Two Fingers Over-lapping Grip — 77
36. Pitch and Run Stance and Address — 78
37. Top of Swing, Pitch and Run — 79
38. Cut Shot Stance and Address — 83
39. Top of Swing for Cut Shot — 84
40. Top of Cut Shot Swing, Side View — 85
41. Unorthodox Cut Shot — 86
42. Side View, Top of Swing of Unorthodox Cut Shot — 87
43. Chip Shot and Run-Up Grip — 89
44. Chip Shot Stance and Address — 90

45. Side View, Chip Shot 91
46. Top of Swing, Chip Shot 92
47. Side View, Chip Shot 93
48. Run-Up Approach Stance and Address 95
49. Back Swing of Run-Up 96
50. Finish of Forward Swing 97
51. Trap Shot Stance and Address 103
52. Side View, Trap Shot Stance and Address 104
53. Top of Back Swing 105
54. Impact 106
55. Left Hand Grip 114
56. Right Hand Grip 115
57. Putting Grip 116
58. Side View of Putting Grip 117
59. Putting Stance and Address 119
60. Putting Stance and Address, Side View 120
61. Another Side View of Putting Stance and Address 121
62. Alternate Putting Stance and Address 122
63. Putter Back Swing 124
64. Putter Forward Swing 125
65. Putter Back Swing, Side View 126
66. Putter Forward Swing, Side View 127

67. Baseball Grip 134
68. Opposed Grip 135
69. Bent Left Arm 136
70. Leaning Over On Toes 137
71. Stiff Arm Swing 138
72. Swaying 139
73. Weight on Left Foot at Top of Swing 140
74. Opening Fingers 141
75. Over Swinging 142
76. Weight on Right Leg at Impact 143
77. Restricted Follow Through 144
78. "Fire and Fall Back" 145
79. Push Shot Stance and Address 151
80. Push Shot Impact 152
81. Intentional Slice Stance and Address 154
82. Intentional Slice Swing 155
83. Intentional Hook Stance and Address 156
84. Finish of Intentional Hook Swing 157
85. Downhill Lie, Stance and Address 158
86. Sidehill Lie, When Standing Below Ball 159
87. Sidehill Lie, Standing Above Ball 160

GOLF AFTER FORTY

The Theory of the Flatfoot Manner

Since the age of forty is generally considered the beginning of middle age, why then should it not also be the psychological time to begin to play down-the-middle golf? Let's forget about those 250 to 300 yard drives we used to get in our younger, slimmer, and more agile days—drives that ended up God knows where. Let's settle now for controlled tee shots of 175 to 210 yards right down the middle, and free from trouble.

Perhaps you think this may not now be possible because your middle-age spread and that cute little rubber tire around your midriff interferes with the beautiful, free, loose-jointed swing and pivot you used to have. If that is what you think, forget it. No matter how roly-poly you are, or get, you can still hit 'em far and straight with less effort than before. Good golf, as well as life, can also begin at forty, if you go about it in the *Flatfoot Manner*. In the following pages I will attempt to elaborate on the *Flatfoot Manner* of playing golf, a method whereby many of the pivoting evils of older and stouter golfers are eliminated. This method will compensate greatly for any loss of muscular co-ordination—brought on either by increased age or weight—so essential to correct timing. The spectacle of the older and more rotund golfers attempting to execute a full and complete pivot is a fearful thing to behold. Because of their lack of suppleness and co-ordination many errors creep into their swings; this is especially true in the downswing.

One of the first compensations made by these golfers in pivoting is to get up on the tip of the left toe at the top of the back swing. This action gets the body around all right, but that is about all that you can say for it. But this incorrect position invites overswinging; and this, in turn, very often causes the fingers of the left hand to open at the top of the swing. The attempt to re-grip on the downswing is the cause of the all-too-frequent "hitting from the top"with the right hand—with all its resultant evils. The tiptoe pivot fails to create the desirable body-spring windup which is acquired in the properly executed pivot.

Also, the return on the downswing from the tiptoe pivot is apt to bring about that "whirling dervish" imitation which causes the player to "wheel" on his shots. Wheeling causes the left foot to be set down with the toe pointing toward the objective, instead of being set down in an across-the-line-of-flight position. Then the clubhead is brought into the ball with a closed or shut face which causes half-smothered hooks or badly pulled shots. Other calamitous results of wheeling and hitting from the top of the swing are collapses of the left arm and the left side. Collapse of the left arm destroys accuracy, and collapse of the left side weakens the power of the stroke since there is nothing left to hit against.

If a close observer will watch Byron Nelson, Sam Snead, or Ben Hogan hit a ball, he will immediately note one particular feature in their play that is the prime requisite to good golf. They set their left heels down hard just as quickly as possible at the start of the down swing. The left foot remains in an across-the-line-of-flight position during the entire forward swing — including the follow through. Bringing the heel down in this manner stiffens and braces the whole left side, giving the player something "to hit against." When you hit a ball with the feeling that you have "hit against a brick wall," you know the ball is going some place *but fast*. That's how little guys like Hogan can bust 'em a mile.

Golf in the *Flatfoot Manner* gives you this braced left side automatically, because the left heel never leaves the ground. At the same time, because of its simplicity of execution, it also eliminates the majority of those swing details which ordinarily confuse the average golfer. He does not have to think of too many things at one time. The right elbow remains tucked in where it belongs, with the left arm nicely stretched out. The head doesn't bob all over the lot; swaying, therefore, is incidentally corrected too. There is less chance of the right shoulder dropping, and this suppresses the tendency to hit behind the ball (taking turf before hitting ball). In fact, there is very little to think about when playing in the *Flatfoot Manner*.

There is nothing new or unusual about flat foot golf—it just needs to be rediscovered every so often. Many of the old time British stars were flat foot golfers, and they could bang them out with the best of them.

In my younger and leaner days, I used a full free pivot with a propensity toward overswinging. Overswinging is less of an evil in the younger player because he has the neural and muscular co-ordination, plus the flexibility, to compensate for it. In the older and more obese player, overswinging is disastrous to good golf and definitely should be avoided. In the last few years I have put on about thirty-five or forty pounds, and all of it seems to have settled in one spot in defiance of all my exercise. It is peculiar how we refuse to believe that after forty our body metabolism is incapable of burning up food at the same rate as it did in our younger days. Excess food after forty usually becomes only one thing—excess avoirdupois. The smart golfer will cut his food intake down about 50 per cent the first moment he notices his tummy bulging.

In earlier days my game was fairly consistent between 75 and 80. Increased age and weight had changed this to an inconsistent range from 78 to 95—I even hit 98 on one terrible occasion. This inconsistency annoyed me so much that I began to experiment with my game. I found I was acquiring a tiptoe pivot, and it occurred to me that the only way to eradicate this evil was by keeping the left foot down completely throughout the entire swing. Upon the very first attempt the shots came off immediately with their old crispness and accuracy, and I decided, then and there, to give this stance a thorough trial.

I started out to groove the swing by shooting two rounds

with the No. 2 iron only, using this club for all shots. Fortunately I encountered only one trap on these rounds and finished with 79 and 80, which I felt was promising for only one club. The last four rounds played that season were played with the full complement of fourteen clubs and the scores were 75, 75, 74, and 76. One of these rounds was played through a torrential rain storm that completely inundated the course. Here the *Flatfoot Manner* saved the day, as I sloshed home the winner of a state service club tournament. No danger of slipping on wet courses when both feet remain flat on the ground. I have persistently adhered to the *Flatfoot Manner* of playing golf ever since, and find my scoring is better now than it was in my younger days.

I have induced many heavy weights to try out the flat foot system, and everyone of them has been keenly enthusiastic about it. So-o-o, we pass it along to you for what it is worth.

However, before we jump into the execution details, let's analyze the scoring possibilities of a round of down-the-middle golf on a good golf course as performed in the *Flatfoot Manner*. I have selected the North Shore Golf Club of Glenview, Illinois, for our example for several reasons. North Shore has been the scene of many national golfing events, and its acreage has been proclaimed by experts a real test of golf. However, North Shore is the same as any other golf course to the extent that it is easy when you're down the middle and tough when you're not. I selected North Shore because it is devoid of water hazards and therefore apt to be more typical of the majority of courses, and also because it is a standard golf course, with four par 3 holes and four par 5's—with none of these either outlandishly tricky nor unreasonably long. Neither has it those fiendishly long 440 or 450 yard par 4 holes that border on par 5 which are constructed for professionals and not for the average golfer. North Shore has three sets of yardages, 6796 for championship play, 6629 on the regular long course, and 6403 on the short course. Since we're not interested in championship play, we will use the regular long course of 6629 yards for our purpose. This distance is perhaps a bit longer than average, but not unreasonably so. All in all, we can generally accept North Shore's layout as being a standard pattern golf course.

Well, here we go flat-footing down the middle of North Shore's verdant fairways. Hope you enjoy the round.

Hole	Yds.	Par	Tee Shot	2nd Shot	3rd Shot	4th Shot	Putts	Score
1	429	4	Driver, 175 yds.	Spoon, 165 yds.	No. 8 iron, 89 yds.		2	5
2	451	5	" " "	" " "	No. 7 " 111 "		2	5
3	157	3	No. 3 iron, 157 "				2	3
4	403	4	Driver, 175 yds.	" " "	No. 9 " 63 "		2	5
5	345	4	" " "	" " "			2	4
6	392	4	" " "	" " "	No. 9 " 52 "		2	5
7	536	5	" " "	" " "	Spoon, 165 "	Pitch 31 yds.	2	6
8	218	3	" " "	No. 9 iron, 43 yds.			2	4
9	396	4	" " "	Spoon, 165 yds.	No. 9 iron, 56 "		2	5

Out 3327 36   Out 18 Out 42

Hole	Yds.	Par	Tee Shot	2nd Shot	3rd Shot	4th Shot	Putts	Score
10	424	4	Driver, 175 yds.	Spoon, 165 yds.	No. 8 iron, 84 yds.		2	5
11	344	4	" " "	" " "			2	4
12	545	5	" " "	" " "	Spoon, 165 yds.	Pitch 40 yds.	2	6
13	166	3	Spoon, 165 yds.				2	3
14	326	4	Driver, 175 yds.	No. 4 iron, 151 yds.	No. 2 iron, 161 yds.		2	4
15	501	5	" " "	Spoon, 165 yds.			2	5
16	152	3	No. 4 iron, 152 "		No. 8 iron, 85 yds.		2	3
17	415	4	Driver, 175 yds.	" " "	No. 7 " 99 "		2	5
18	429	4	" " "		No. 9 iron, 43 "		2	5

In 3302 36   In 18 In 40

Out 3327 36
Total 6629 72   Total 36 82

A score of 82 on any golf course represents a fairly decent businessman's count in any league. In fact, anything under 85 should be considered excellent golf, for it entitles you to become an "A" Class member under the existing club handicapping systems. Less than 5 per cent of the country's golfers can qualify as Class "A" players. Yet it shouldn't be too difficult to crash the gates into this exclusive society.

Let's review our mythical paper tour and see if we can't discover the key to "A" Class scoring. In this ghost round, of course, we counted on every shot being played perfectly as per schedule, and therefore we made no allowances for excursions into the rough, or for traps or other hazards. However, to offset some of these errors which occur in every round of golf, we have made several compensations. Note that we have been satisfied with 175 yard tee shots. No doubt several of our drives would be nearer 200 yards, thereby making the second and third shots easier. An average of 175 off the tee will probably take care of some of the yardage lost on dubbed drives. Also note we have been equally satisfied with 165 yard spoon shot seconds. Many of these would probably exceed this distance, making the third shot merely a chip in those instances. We haven't mentioned the use of a brassie in our round, because the writer believes this is a good club to leave at home or use off the tee only. The spoon is a much better club to use through the fairway for the average golfer. Being shorter, with a greater loft, it gets the ball up into the air more quickly. Fairway conditions are not generally good enough for brassie use. Tight lies are more confidently handled with the Nos. 3 or 4 woods. After all, there is only a difference of about 10 yards in distance between the brassie and spoon—which is nothing to worry about, especially since the spoon is the more consistently dependable weapon.

Where we have a third or fourth shot to the green we have not had to use anything longer or stronger than a No. 7 iron, and the longest distance negotiated with this club was 111 yards on the 3rd hole. This distance and all the others with the Nos. 8 and 9 irons are all played well within these clubs' capabilities, so there has been no need to press any club for full distance. Pressing for distance ruins more shots than any other fault. Maximum distances on these irons are usually rated as following, No. 7, 135 yds., No. 8, 120 yds., No. 9, 100 yds.

Great emphasis should be placed on the short game by the over forty golfer. In order to maintain a class A rating he must become highly proficient with the short irons, and a master of all shots from 125 yards in. He must not only be able to hit the green from these distances, but he also must place the shots somewhere near the pin. Simply shooting for the green is not enough. Always plan the shot so as to leave a one putter. The short game is a cinch for the *Flatfoot Manner*. It is especially efficacious in approaching, since little or no pivoting is required in these short pitches and chip shots.

Now we come to the most important subject of our whole round — *Putting*. Often have we heard the statement that matches and tournaments are won on the green, and it is certainly true. Tournament players vary little from tee to green, and consequently the player who is "hot" with his putter is generally the winner. Par scoring allows for 36 putts per round which is generally about 50 per cent of the strokes used. In our ghost round you will note that we, too, allowed this maximum putting total. But within this total lies also the opportunity of saving several strokes to compensate again for other errors along the route. However, 36 putts per round is not a really good putting total for Class A players with handicaps from 6 to 11 or B class up to 14. Players in this group should rarely have more than 30 to 32 putts to the round. Due to the fact that they may be generally short of the green with their second and third shots, they are very often in position to run in simple approach shots close to the hole for one putters. Quite often a 10 handicapper will outscore a scratch player with this method. The scratch player is constantly striving to hit the green with his second or third shots, depending on the par of the hole. If he happens to be "off the beam" on a particular day, he may find himself constantly scrambling out of traps and other trouble. The 10 handicapper is satisfied to be a bit short of the objective and therein lies the secret of his scoring success. His motto is , "*always stay short of trouble*." Let this sensible maxim be the future guide for the over forty golfer who desires to shoot consistently good golf. Let's play golf with our heads instead of our backs. Don't take chances with trouble on a golf course. Don't try quick rising, high flying shots over trees and bushes in your line, unless you are far enough away to give the ball a chance to get up. If there is any doubt about making such a shot come off, then don't try it. Play the alternate safety shot of chipping back into the fairway and taking your chances of getting on close enough for one putt to neutralize the penalizing chip shot.

Now back to putting. Every over forty golfer who aspires to good golf must become a maestro of putting. He should consider his putter as the Stradivarius of all his golfing tools. He should give it the attention and reverence that a concert violinist would give a genuine Strad, for it is capable of playing many a sweet tune on the golfing green. It has been said that good putters are born and not made. I disagree with that philosophy. Some putters, of course, will always be better than others, just as there are geniuses in all lines of endeavor. But, this should not discourage anyone from becoming a better than average putter. There are certain fundamentals and putting tricks that will give consistently uniform results. These can be mastered by anyone with a little effort.

I consider putting my special forte in golf, and I have spent a great deal of time on putting clocks experimenting with this phase of the game. These efforts have been rewarded by a steadiness on the greens that rarely exceeds 30 putts per round. There have been many instances of 24, 25, and 26 putts per round with a low of 22 upon one occasion. In fact, Sunday, (Oct. 22nd, 1944) at the Elmhurst Country Club, my home club, I gave my opponents a demonstration of *The Hattstrom "IN-LINE" Technique* of putting, which cost the boys a few dimes when I went around in 25 putts, 12 on the first 9 and 13 on the last. And, I missed three footers at the 1st and 9th holes. The majority of these putts were of the 5 and 10 foot varieties with three or four exceeding 20 feet. Digest completely the section on putting, it will pay dividends if you will but give it a chance.

The Grip

The Grip

THERE ARE TWO GRIPS RECOMMENDED. For those who have hands and fingers of normal size and strength the Vardon overlapping grip (2)* is suggested. If the hands are small or weak, the two-handed grip is preferable (3). This grip is ideal for many women. In both grips the club is held in the fingers and not in the palm of the hand. In the overlapping grip the little finger of the right hand overlaps or rests on the index finger of the left hand. The thumb of the left hand nestles in the palm of the right. In both grips the V formed by thumb and index fingers on both hands points to the right shoulder when stance is taken. Grip firmly with left hand and lightly with right, but firm does not mean tightly. Tightness means stiffness, and stiffness means locked arms and wrists which destroy muscular flexibility. Only grip firmly enough to maintain control of the club throughout the entire swing.

* The numbers in parentheses throughout the text refer to illustrations.

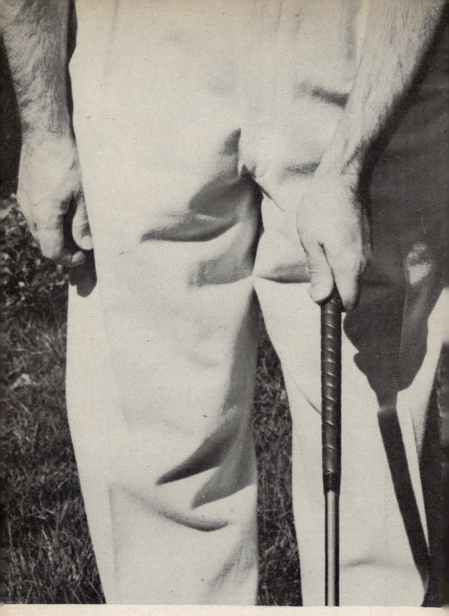

1. LEFT HAND GRIP. The V formed by the thumb and index finger points approximately to the right shoulder. This V should be kept closed during entire swing. Keeping it closed prevents club shaft from falling into crotch. Grip firmly with left hand but not tightly. Tightness locks muscles.

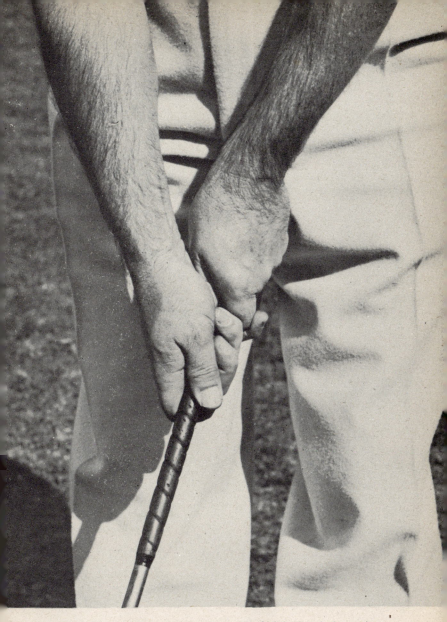

2. THE VARDON OVERLAPPING GRIP. V of right hand also points to right shoulder. Little finger of right hand overlaps or rests on index finger of left hand. Grip of right hand should be on light side to prevent it from overpowering the left since right hand is usually the stronger member. This is also one of the reasons for the overlapping grip, since there will be only three fingers of the right hand on the shaft against four of the left hand.

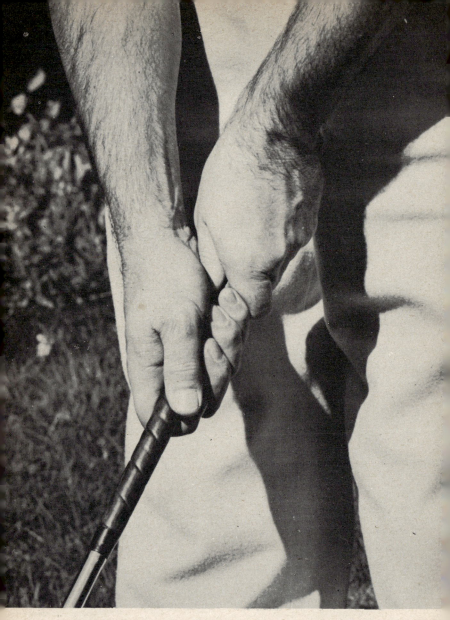

3. THE TWO-HANDED GRIP. V's point to right shoulder, and all fingers of both hands are on the shaft. This grip is ideal for golfers with small or weak hands. This is a fine grip for the average woman. In all grips club is held in the fingers, and not in the palms of the hands.

The Stance

The Stance

A SQUARE or slightly closed stance is used. For those on the lean side who can turn freely at the waist the square stance is recommended (4). For those of ample girth the closed stance is preferable (6). The closed stance insures hitting from the inside, and less pivoting is required. There is also more power in the hit from this stance. In the closed stance the right foot is drawn back about three inches from the line of flight. Shoulders and hips should be in a parallel position to the toes whichever stance is used.

Left foot is planted firmly, flatly, and squarely across the line of flight. Right toe is turned out slightly to the right, facilitating a better hip turn. Body in fairly erect position, with hands and arms hanging practically straight down—there should be no stretching or reaching for ball. Settle back on heels with weight evenly distributed between both feet. Spread feet apart the width of shoulders. Because of the fairly erect position, ball is played in a bit closer than otherwise.

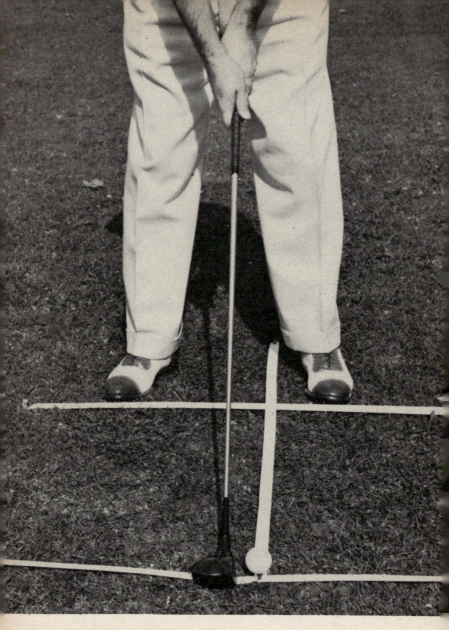

4. SQUARE STANCE. Left foot is planted firmly, flatly, and squarely across line of flight. Right toe is also on parallel line, but is turned out slightly to the right to facilitate a better hip turn. Weight evenly distributed between both feet, with predominance on heels. Knees slightly flexed.

5. SIDE VIEW OF SQUARE STANCE.

6. CLOSED STANCE. Left foot is in same position, but right foot is drawn back two or three inches from line of flight. This is the preferred stance for older and heavier golfers as it gives a better body turn on the backswing. It also helps to keep swing from the inside-out.

8. OPEN STANCE. Here left foot is drawn back two or three inches from line of flight, and right foot is nearly square to the line. This stance is to be avoided by older and heavier players as it usually brings the swing in from the outside and causes sliced balls. This stance should only be used where an intentional slice is desired.

9. SIDE VIEW OF OPEN STANCE.

The Woods

The Woods

IN THE DRIVE off the tee with the woods the ball is played from a point slightly inside of the left heel. Ball is struck squarely in the back and slightly on the up stroke. On a brassie shot from the fairway the ball is placed about halfway between the left heel and the center and the ball is struck squarely in the back. For spoon and cleek shots (Nos. 3 and 4 woods), the ball is played from center position, and the ball is struck with a slightly descending blow similar to the irons. Back swing is started by turning the left shoulder, letting it control the left arm entirely. Grip firmly with left hand, and be extremely conscious of left hand control throughout the entire swing both up and down. Right hand will automatically come in at the right time of its own accord. Keep the clubhead low, practically dragging it along the turf with the hands leading slightly ahead, allowing the left-shoulder-and-body-turn more or less to take the club up for you automatically (11). This type of back swing stretches the left arm well out, and increases the arc of the swing. A lifted club shortens the arc, and is conducive to right hand control—which is detrimental to power and accuracy. Body turn will come at the waist and hips with a slight transference of weight to the right foot at the top of the swing, left foot still remaining flat on the ground. Left knee will fall in slightly towards the right leg. In this position there will be felt a distinct body-spring windup effect, which, when properly unleashed on the downspring, produces plenty of power.

At the top of the backswing, a full swing with the woods puts the club shaft in a horizontal position parallel to the ground

(See 13). Now here is the million dollar secret of good golf! Pay strict attention to the following statement and remember it on every shot. *At top of backswing, club shaft should be in an across-the-line-of-flight position!* For example, using the hours 12 and 6 on the clock face as the line-of-flight, club shaft should be in approximately a 1 to 7 o'clock position (14, 22, 23). This position insures hitting from the inside, and enables you to hit the ball hard should you so desire. Many golfers believe that if the shaft is in the line-of-flight position at the top of the back swing they will then hit the ball on a straight line. This is an erroneous thought. At the beginning of the downswing the body leads slightly ahead, bringing the left shoulder around a bit. This slight turn to the left will bring the shaft around from the line-of-flight position to an approximate 11 to 5 position—from which the club will be swung from the outside-in. This action produces those beautiful slices. When the shaft is in the 1 to 7 o'clock across-the-line-of-flight position at the top of the backswing, the slightly leading body turn brings the shaft into a position a little past 12 to 6. This brings the clubhead into the ball from the inside, and delivers either a straight ball or one with a slight hook. No doubt you've heard the pros tell their slicing students who fear out-of-bounds on the right to try purposely to hit a ball-out-of-bounds. When this was tried the student was amazed to see the ball fly straight and true down the middle of the fairway. The pro was merely trying to get him to swing from the inside-out. So, remember, at the top of the back swing have the club shaft *across the line of flight!* You can usually tell when you are doing this correctly, since you can catch a glimpse of the clubhead out of the corner of your left eye at the top of the swing. When shaft is in the line-of-flight or in the out-side-in position (11 to 5 o'clock), clubhead cannot be seen with the left eye.

At the top of the backswing, both hands and wrists should be practically under the shaft. This position keeps the right elbow from wandering too far away, and also puts the left hand in a powerful hitting position. The left hand in this position keeps the club face wide open, with the toe of the club pointing to the ground at the top of the swing (13). This is an extremely important point. Embryo golfers usually shy away from the open face method of hitting a golf ball because they fear the face will not close on the downswing. They become more or less "shut face" golfers with all of the difficulties that produces. They're the boys who are constantly pulling and smothering their shots. Their No. 7 iron shots have the trajectory of a No. 3 iron. The open face system is the only real method for combined power and accuracy. The flail of the wrists acting as a hinge at the point of impact causes the face to close automatically with a terrific flick, producing tremendous power with little effort.

Start the downswing slowly with the left hand and keep the club face open by bringing the club down close to the body and leading it down with the heel of the left hand. Feel that you're hitting the ball with the heel of the left hand and not the back of the hand. This action will also help you to hit from the inside-out — the goal of all good golfers. Shift the weight over to the left foot, and hit against the braced left side. Be sure and follow through all the way. Don't be in a hurry to hit the ball. It will still be there when the club head gets down to it.

The swing should be of the upright variety. The flat swing is almost as dead today as the proverbial dodo. There are good reasons for 90 per cent of modern pros to use the upright swing. There is a greater margin of safety. This is because the upright swinger is swinging in a groove which is somewhat parallel to the line of flight, giving more accuracy. The flat swinger must hit the ball at almost dead center of his arc. Remember—*the swing is the thing*. Swing, swing, swing. Don't hit! Sweep the ball away in wood shots off the tee.

10. THE DRIVE ADDRESS. Body bent over only enough to accommodate length of club and distance to ball. Favor an erect position. Let hands and arms hang down naturally (7). Do not stretch or reach for ball. Hands directly in front, neither ahead nor behind clubhead. Weight back on heels. Shoulders and hips in same plane as stance (toe line). Clubhead soled flat, neither toe nor heel off ground. Ball played from a position slightly inside of left heel.

11. THE DRAG BACK. Let left shoulder take club back. This will make the hands lead the clubhead slightly, and at same time keep it on the ground for a considerable distance in the backswing. Action will increase swing arc and prevent lifting of club.

12. THE UPSWING. The drag back has created a nicely stretched out left arm. Wrists are now turning and face of club is opening up. Left shoulder and hips still turning. Weight shifting to right foot and leg. Left foot still flat on ground. Head Steady.

44

13. TOP OF BACK SWING. Left shoulder is now all the way around so that left eye is looking directly over shoulder at ball. Hips well around and back is practically facing toward objective. Left foot still flat on ground and left knee has fallen in toward right leg. Club shaft in horizontal position parallel with the ground. This is proper position for full swing. Do not let clubhead drop below this horizontal position or you will overswing. Note club face is now wide open and toe of clubhead is pointing to ground. This puts the hands well under shaft and in a powerful hitting position.

45

14. TOP OF BACK SWING, SIDE VIEW. Right elbow has been kept well in, and hands are in good hitting position with wrists properly cocked. *Take special notice of angle of club shaft in relation to line of flight! It is in the 1 to 7 o'clock position, across the line of flight.* This position is extremely important to good golf as it will bring the clubhead into the ball from the inside-out. (See also 22, 23, 24, and 25 for further illustration of this all-important point.)

15. HALF WAY DOWN. Left arm taking club down on inside and close to body. Right elbow now well tucked in. Heel and not back of left hand bringing club down. Wrists still cocked. Club face wide open. Head steady and weight shifting over to left foot and leg.

17. THREE QUARTERS DOWN. Weight now well over on left foot and leg. Left arm straight, right elbow in. Wrists beginning to uncock. Heel of left hand still leading clubhead down and club face still open. Get into habit of feeling that you are hitting the ball with the heel of the left hand. Right hand just beginning to get into stroke. Do not consciously hit with right hand; let left do it all. Right hand will come in automatically.

18. IMPACT. Weight now completely over on left foot and leg, and hit is being made against braced left side. Right heel now coming up slightly. Head still in original position. Left arm is straight, and right now also straightens into shot. Club face still a bit open going into ball and will close during impact.

19. IMPACT, SIDE VIEW.

20. THE FOLLOW THROUGH. Right arm remains straight clear through and beyond impact. Head is still maintaining original position, but will now begin to turn with follow through. Stroke has been made against braced left side, and left foot has remained in original across-line-of-flight position. Right hand is now rolling over immediately after impact. Follow through of clubhead will in itself bring the body around after it.

21. FINISH OF SWING. A full and complete follow through is merely an end result, and an indication that the entire stroke has been made correctly from the beginning. Body has turned completely and now faces objective. Note that left foot is still in original position, with weight rolled over onto outer edge.

22. 1 TO 7 O'CLOCK POSITION. This view was taken from rear and above to illustrate proper angle of shaft at top of swing. In order to swing properly from the inside out the club must be in this across-the-line-of-flight position at the top of swing. This action brings the left shoulder completely around to where left eye looks directly over shoulder at ball.

23. 1 TO 7 O'CLOCK POSITION, SIDE VIEW.

24. 12 TO 6 O'CLOCK POSITION. Here club shaft is in same plane as the line of flight. Hitting from this position will cause a slice.

25. 11 TO 5 O'CLOCK POSITION. Body has failed to turn sufficiently on back swing and swing will be definitely from the outside-in. This type of swing produces real slices, sometimes almost in boomerang form.

The Irons

The Irons

A THREE-QUARTER SWING is sufficient for any iron (30). For all irons, except in cut and trap shots, assume the square stance. In our flat foot system we are attempting to standardize both stance and swing for all shots. The fewer details we have to think about, the more automatic and precise we will become. In the usual method of instruction for iron play, the recommendation has been to use a square stance for the Nos. 1 and 2 irons, and from thereon up an increasingly open stance is advised so that with the No. 9 niblick you will find the left foot drawn back to where the toe is practically pointing to the objective. The only trouble with this open stance method is that ever so often the shot will come off on the toe line, and the ball will wind up considerably to the left of the objective. The theory of the open stance pitch to the green is that it produces a slightly left to right trajectory, with a slight cut on the ball which will cause it to stop rather quickly. The shot, therefore, has to be aimed slightly to the left of the pin. It is also claimed that the left side is out of the way, and doesn't interfere with the execution of the stroke. For the older player, however, the open stance will probably produce more slices than anything else. A No. 9 niblick can be played just as effectively from a square stance as from an open. Its slightly right to left action on a high pitch produces a driving down effect which stops the ball on the green just as effectively as the modified cut shot from the open stance. The part I like about the square stance is that you are always in line with your objective, and need not make any adjustments or compensations for it.

For a No. 2 or 3 iron shot the ball should be played about midway between the feet (26). From thereon up the ball should be moved gradually back toward the right foot until finally with the No. 9 iron the ball is played opposite the right heel (27). Each succeeding iron also brings the ball closer in according to the length of the club shaft.

Irons are played somewhat differently than are the woods. Woods call for more or less sweeping strokes. Iron shots are definitely more of a hit, and the stroke is played more crisply— the ball being hit "down" and through. All irons should be hit with a descending blow in such a way that the turf or divot is taken after the ball is struck (34). This club action produces both backspin and control. The turf straightens out the blade, and hence gives more accuracy. Don't be afraid to bang the ball down as though you were attempting to drive it into the ground. The natural loft of the club head will send the ball up without any additional help. Too many golfers think that to loft a ball into the air you must help it up by actually hitting it up. Golf is a game of opposites. If you want a ball to go up, you hit it down. If down, you hit it up. To send a ball to the right, you hit out to the left. To send one to the left, you hit out to the right.

The grip with the left hand should be a trifle firmer with the irons than with the woods. Keep the left arm straight but not rigid, and also well stretched out. Keep the blade open all the way down to the ball, and feel that you are actually hitting the ball with the heel, not the back, of the hand. Bring the left arm down close to the body and keep the right elbow tucked in. Be sure that the left hand has complete control of the club both up and down. The right hand will come in automatically, so you should keep the right hand grip on the light side—just feel the thumb and index finger holding the club only. Let the left shoulder take the club back. This insures getting into proper hitting position at the top of the swing. When the club is taken back and up by the hands and arms only, there is always the possibility of the left shoulder not getting around. The swing will then come from the outside. Keep the clubhead low in the backswing.

Never slug with an iron—play well within yourself. If you are at all in doubt as to whether you can make the distance with a particular club or not, change immediately to the next longer club and swing easily. Since 80 per cent of all approach shots from 135 to 175 yards are generally short of their objective, get into the habit of shooting for the top of the flag. Under this plan you may occasionally go over the green but there's a great satisfaction in knowing that at least you were hole high on the shot. Generally there is very little trouble in back of a green anyway, and it is just as easy to chip back to the hole as it is to chip up to it.

26. MID-IRON STANCE. Use either square or slightly closed stance. Ball played practically in center, or very slightly forward of center, if preferred. Slightly firmer left hand grip than with woods, but still not on the tight side. Hands in a position slightly ahead of clubhead. Weight evenly distributed on both feet with predominance on heels. Knees slightly flexed.

27. NIBLICK STANCE. Use square stance with feet closer together and nearer to ball. Ball played well back, practically off right heel. Hands still in center of body but now are considerably ahead of clubhead. Ball is struck on a descending blow, that is, ball is taken first and divot after. (See 34.)

28. STANCE AND ADDRESS FOR NO. 5 IRON. Ball played slightly back of center. Hands in center and a bit ahead of clubhead.

29. SIDE VIEW OF NO. 5 IRON STANCE AND ADDRESS. Hands in close and not reaching for ball. Weight back on heels.

30. TOP OF IRON SWING. A three-quarters swing is sufficient fo
any and all irons. This is the top of a swing for a No. 5 iron. Feet flat o
ground.

1. TOP OF IRON SWING, SIDE VIEW. Left shoulder well around, left arm stretched out and right elbow in. Club face wide open with toe of clubhead pointing to ground. Hands well under shaft with wrists cocked. Left hand in control with heel of hand in powerful hitting position. Swing will come from inside.

32. HALF WAY DOWN. Left arm straight, right elbow in. Blade stil
wide open and wrists are just beginning to uncock. Left hand in contro
with heel of left hand leading into ball.

70

33. INSTANT BEFORE IMPACT. Left arm is straight and right also straightens out. Left side braced and weight has moved over onto left foot and leg. Head still in original position with left eye over ball. Clubface still open and just beginning to close.

34. TAKING OF DIVOT. This is a posed picture showing position of ball before stroke was made. The ball being hit "down" on a descending blow it is therefore struck first and the blade continues on down and through to take the divot in front of the ball. This picture illustrates a full divot taken by a niblick shot. Divots should be taken with practically all the irons. Size of divot taken will be corresponding less in the longer irons, the No. 2 iron taking but very little turf.

The Short Game

The Short Game

As MENTIONED BEFORE, the after forty golfer must become the master of the short game if he desires to become or remain a Class A golfer. The *Flatfoot Manner* lends itself superbly to this phase of the game as little or no pivot is required for shots of 75 yards or less. The most important item to remember in the short game is to let the club do the work. Club must be swung and not jerked or jabbed. The ball will stay in line when despatched by a swinging club, but it may go in any direction when stabbed. Keep the feet close together with the same square stance. Be thoroughly relaxed with knees slightly flexed. Firm grip with left hand.

In the pitches with the Nos. 7, 8, and 9 irons where left hand control is extremely essential, it is sometimes advantageous to overlap two fingers of the right hand instead of one (35). This grip will help to keep the right hand from overpowering the left. At the same time it will make the player definitely more conscious of left hand dominance in the stroke. There will also be more feel of the clubhead in the swing.

Keep club face open and swing slightly from inside of the line of flight. There are two types of shots that should be mastered in the short game, the abrupt stop and the running shot. The stop shot is made by putting plenty of backspin on the ball, and this is created by striking the ball with a crisply descending blow. Ball should be played opposite right heel. This insures ball being hit "down" in such a way as to take the turf or divot after hitting ball. In this type of shot the ball carries most of the distance and has very little run after striking the green. In fact, a ball with a heavy back spin will very often jump backwards from its landing spot—depending on the surface and texture of the green.

The running shot is more of a low pitch and run shot. Ball carries half to two-thirds of the distance and runs the rest of the way. Running shots can be successfully made with any iron from Nos. 4 to 7. Ball is played from a position slightly inside of left heel (36 and 37). A one-quarter to one-half swing is sufficient for these shots. The ball is not hit "down" as in other iron shots, but is struck squarely in the back and slightly on the upswing. This creates the overspin that makes the ball run. The stroke is more of a "slinging" clubhead hit. If more than normal run is desired this can be had by turning the right hand over just as clubhead comes in contact with the ball. The roll-over action of the clubhead increases overspin on the ball.

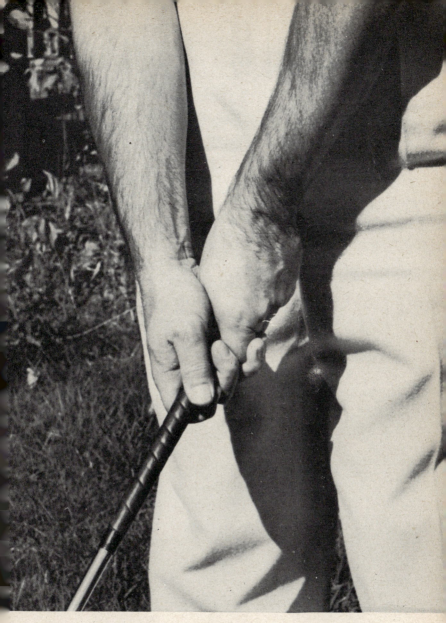

35. TWO FINGERS OVERLAPPING GRIP. Full pitches to the green with Nos. 7, 8, and 9 irons demand positive left hand control. This can be acquired by some players by overlapping two fingers instead of one. In this way the right hand will be kept from overpowering the left. There will also be more feel of clubhead in this grip.

36. PITCH AND RUN STANCE AND ADDRESS. This shot can be played with any iron from Nos. 4 to 7. Square stance is used with ball being played slightly inside left heel.

37. TOP OF SWING, PITCH AND RUN. Ball is not hit "down" as in regular iron shots, but is struck squarely in back and slightly on upswing. Stroke is more of a "slinging" clubhead hit.

The Cut Shot

THE "CUT" SHOT to the average golfer comes under the heading of trick shots and in the same category as intentional hooks and slices. He leaves these shots to the experts and the pros to execute. However, I believe any Class A or low Class B player is capable of fairly consistently making the cut shot. It is not difficult to execute, and it is a highly valuable shot to have in the bag when needed.

A cut shot is a quick rising, quick stopping shot, with little or no run on the ball when alighting on the green. What little run it may have will be from left to right so the shot is generally aimed slightly to the left of the hole. The quick stopping action on the ball comes from a combination of side and under spin imparted by the club. The cut shot can be played with almost any lofted club to a certain degree, but it is best exemplified with the Nos. 7, 8, and 9 irons. The Nos. 8 and 9 irons are usually used in this shot because of their higher loft, and because their wider faces can be laid back still farther if necessary.

The value of the cut shot comes in the ability to surmount objects like trees, bushes, houses, fences, bunkers, traps, and so on, when they are in the line of flight and in close proximity. It is also useful in playing from beyond a trap to the green where the hole is placed close to the near edge.

In the *Flatfoot Manner* of playing golf we deviate from the regular square or closed stance on only two shots—the cut and the trap shots. These are played with an open stance with the left foot drawn back about four inches from the line of flight. The reason for open stances in these strokes is that the ball is struck from the outside-in—in the same manner as in playing for an intentional slice. The *Flatfoot Manner* is ideal for execution of the cut shot, since practically no pivot is required. The ball is played slightly inside of the left heel. The swing is more upright than for any other type shot. Keep the blade wide open. Take the club back with the left hand and slightly on the outside of a line, parallel with your toes, pointing to the left of the objective. For this shot it is not necessary to get the hands any higher than waist level on the backswing. Start the club down with the left hand and bring it down smartly from the outside-in, cutting the blade directly underneath the ball. Go all the way through to a full follow through.

Ball and turf must be struck precisely at the same time. Do not attempt this shot on hard or bare ground as clubhead must go through turf directly underneath the ball. The shot is best executed when the ball-sets up well in grass. Where a ball has to travel but a very short distance and you have a lofty bunker to carry immediately in front of you, there is an alternate method of playing the cut shot (41 and 42). This stroke might correctly be labeled a trick shot. Yet it is easy to manipulate. A square stance is used, with all the weight on the left foot. The entire weight remains on the left foot throughout the entire swing; the right merely acts as a supporter of balance. The ball is played in close and is placed about three or four inches to the *Left* of the left toe. The ball must have a fairly good lie for this shot. Use only the regular No. 9 niblick and lay the face back wide open. Take the clubhead back on the outside and bring it down crisply, cutting underneath and across the ball. The ball will virtually jump up perpendicularly and drop dead upon alighting. A full swing won't send this ball any farther than ten to twenty feet. In fact, this shot can be made in such a manner that you can actually reach out and catch the ball in your hand on the descent. The beauty of the cut stroke is that it is more or less of an all-out shot. You might get equal results from some other type of stroke under similar conditions, but it would mean playing very delicate little shots with great dexterity. Only the golfer who plays everyday has that fine a touch. You don't have to baby a cut shot. One can really go after it with more or less reckless abandon, feeling sure the shot will come off safely. The golfer who hasn't played golf all winter and comes out in spring for his first game rarely has much trouble with his long game. This is because he can use a full swing for these shots, and his muscles are not called upon for fine adjustment. It is in the short game that the infrequent golfer suffers. To have the short-game touch, the muscles and nerves must be conditioned by repetition. This calls for a good deal of practice.

This fact is one of the reasons the American style of play calls for so many clubs in the bag. In the olden days, and especially in England, a set of clubs consisted of two woods, a mid-iron, a mashie, a mashie niblick and a putter. Intermediate shots were made by playing half strokes with the next longer club. Half strokes require a nicety of touch we do not have or see today. The modern American golfer wants to bang everything; no sissy shots for him. So the matched set of clubs was born, graduated from Nos. 1 to 5 in woods and 1 to 9 in irons. They are all supposed to swing the same, so you merely select the right club for the distance and smash away. Practically the same length of swing is used for the No. 9 iron as for the No. 2. And we have to admit readily that great results have been obtained in this system of club handling.

Practice the cut shot at every opportunity. It will save many a stroke for you. Besides you'll get a great kick out of a well executed cut shot—it's different.

38. CUT SHOT STANCE AND ADDRESS. Open stance is used with left foot drawn back and left toe pointing out. Right foot square. Ball played just inside of left heel. Club face open and hands slightly ahead of clubhead.

39. TOP OF SWING FOR CUT SHOT. Feet flat on ground and very little body turn. Straight left arm and cocked wrists. Club face wide open; swing will come slightly from outside.

40. TOP OF CUT SHOT SWING, SIDE VIEW. Ball and turf should be struck simultaneously with the blade cutting across the ball from outside in. This action will impart a combination of side and under spin on the ball.

41. UNORTHODOX CUT SHOT. Where a quick rising short distance shot is desired, this "trick" cut shot comes in handy. Square stance is used with practically all the weight on the left foot, right merely supporting balance. Ball played beyond left toe three or four inches and rather close in. Club face laid back wide open. Use No. 9 niblick.

42. SIDE VIEW, TOP OF SWING OF UNORTHODOX CUT SHOT. Club is taken back with left hand, and definitely on the outside. No body pivot at all. Very upright swing. Bring club down smartly from extreme outside and cut across directly underneath ball. Shot is best executed when back of clubhead is more or less "slapped" down on turf.

The Chip Shot

CHIP SHOTS ARE SHORT approaches from surrounding areas of a green. They play a highly important roll in scoring. The deft chipper will have many a one-putt green, and will often hole out these little shots. Chip shots are wrist shots—almost the same as in putting, except that the ball is struck crisply on the down stroke. Assume a square stance with feet close together (44). Take a low grip on the club, with hands ahead of clubhead. Take the club back slowly with the left hand and wrist only, and bring it forward with the right. This stroke must be executed slowly, smoothly, and firmly. Grip should be on firm side. Finish the stroke with clubhead facing toward hole. Chips are best accomplished with the Nos. 7, 8, or 9 irons. Here's a chip tip that works well with some players. Use the reverse overlap grip similar to the one used in putting. Overlap the index finger of left hand over little finger of right. This puts the control in the right hand, which is desirable since chip shots are normally right hand shots (43).

43. CHIP SHOT AND RUN-UP GRIP. This is a very efficient grip for the short game around the green. Since chips and run-ups are more or less elongated putts, the stroke is made more satisfactorily with right hand dominance. The grip pictured here is the reverse overlap. Grip with left hand should be on light side, right quite firm.

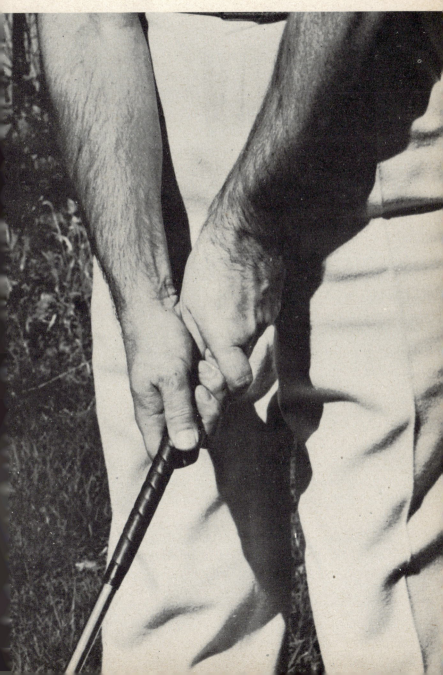

44. CHIP SHOT STANCE AND ADDRESS. Feet close together, square stance. Ball played opposite left heel. Take shortened grip on club shaft. Hands ahead of clubhead. Clubhead square to line.

45. SIDE VIEW, CHIP SHOT. Hands held well in and ball played up close. Knees flexed and weight well back on heels.

46. TOP OF SWING, CHIP SHOT. Stroke is practically a wrist shot, very little arm movement necessary. Club taken back with left hand and forward stroke made with right hand. Firm grip with right.

47. SIDE VIEW, CHIP SHOT. From camera angle of this picture it appears forward swing is coming well from the inside, but actually the chip stroke is made practically in the line of flight similar to a long putt stroke. Hit through ball crisply and firmly, and finish with club-head low to the ground and facing squarely to hole.

The Run-Up Shot

FOR SHOTS OFF THE FRINGE of the green with a clear pathway to the hole a different stroke is recommended. Take the same stance as before, standing fairly erect (48). Use a No. 4 iron and reverse overlap grip. Play ball off left toe. This is also purely a wrist stroke. Take club back with the left hand and keep clubhead low to the ground. Take it straight back from ball along the line to the hole. Bring club forward with right hand, and with a low sweeping stroke go right through the ball and finish with clubhead still on line and pointing to the hole. Play stroke slowly but firmly. Stroke is more of a swinging sweep than a hit. Ball will have more run on it than in the chip-type stroke.

Since shots off the fringe are nothing more than elongated putts, there is no reason why the putting stroke could not also be used effectively for these small shots. The Hattstrom *"In-Line"* Technique of putting can be successfully used on these shots and would assure the same accuracy in direction. The Hattstrom *"In-Line"* Run-up club was especially designed for these shots. It has the loft of a No. 4 iron with an extra heavy head to create pendulum stroking effect, which prevents tendency to hit or jerk club off line. It has an upright lie, like a putter, to induce swinging *"In Line."*

48. RUN-UP APPROACH STANCE AND ADDRESS. Feet close together and body fairly erect. Ball played just inside left toe. Use No. 4
iron for this shot. Reverse overlap grip, same as for chip shots.

49. BACK SWING OF RUN-UP. Run-ups are purely wrist shots. Club taken back with left hand directly on the line. Blade square on both backward and forward swing. Keep clubhead low to ground.

96

50. FINISH OF FORWARD SWING. Club brought forward with right hand. With low sweeping stroke, go through ball and finish with club-head on line, blade still square. Play stroke slowly but firmly.

97

The Trap Shot

The Trap Shot

THE GOOD GOLFER thinks of only one thing when he's in the sand trap. To get out in one stroke! Of course he'll try to get close to the hole with the shot, but uppermost in his mind is the determination to get out in one shot. He doesn't want to spend the day in a trap simulating a hacking snake killer.

There are many varieties of trap shots, but day in and day out, the only one, good, safe, reliable shot is the explosion shot. So we will confine our remarks on trap shots entirely to the explosion. The average golfer shies away from the explosion shot with a great deal of fear. He looks upon any one who can properly execute this stroke as some sort of golfing wizard. And yet the way an explosion shot is made today, it is one of the easiest shots in the game. The answer to the problem is to be found in the modern heavy sand iron or wedge. You just can't miss with this bludgeon. I have been using the wedge for the past four or five years, and in that time I have not failed to emerge from a trap on the first try more than three or four times. Being in a trap doesn't ruffle me a bit. I actually enjoy playing an explosion shot because the wedge gives you that sort of confidence. If you don't possess one of these trouble savers, I beg you to purchase one at your earliest opportunity. It will be an investment that will pay off in big dividends and one you'll never regret. You will use it for many other short shots from the rough also.

Take care in your selection of the wedge to see that you get one with a straight leading edge instead of a curved one. The straight edge will be more accurate in your hands. The

curved edge type extends about one-eighth to one-quarter
inch more forward at the center than the straight edge variety.
This small amount may seem infinitesimal, but it is amazing th
difference it makes in accuracy down at the ball. Be sure you
select the heavy wedge with the big flange. Avoid the so-called
double-duty type of niblick which is a cross between the wedg
and the regular No. 9 niblick. Get the heavy one—the heavie
the better.

The explosion shot is played beautifully in the *Flatfoo
Manner*, for little or no pivot is required, and the *Flatfoo
Manner* anchors your feet solidly in the sand, which is abso
lutely essential in the explosion shot. Take an open stanc
with left foot drawn back about three inches (51). Wiggl
your feet around to get a good firm foundation. Ball is playe
slightly inside left heel and fairly close in, since this is to b
quite an upright swing shot. Grip very firmly and keep th
face of the club open. Take club back slightly on the outsid
with the left hand. Hands at top of back swing need not b
higher than waist level (53). Now here is the secret of success
ful explosion-shot making. First observe the texture of th
sand and determine the distance behind the ball where the club
head is to go into the sand. When you have selected this spot
glue your eyes to this spot only! Completely disregard the bal
altogether, see only this spot. Watch this spot continuousl
until the clubhead has banged down into it and gone right on
through under the ball. Play the stroke crisply, but be sure t
let the heavy clubhead do the work. Resolve to let it go all th
way through to a complete finish. Don't baby this shot at any
time, and don't try to check or stop the club at any point in th
forward swing. Aim slightly to left of hole. The amount o
sand you take is governed entirely by the distance you wish t
travel. The striking spot behind the ball may be anywhere from
a half inch to four or five inches, depending on the texture an
condition of the sand and the distance to go. Increase distanc
behind the ball for soft sand and decrease it for hard or we
sand.

51. TRAP SHOT STANCE AND ADDRESS. Open stance used with left foot drawn back three or four inches. Wiggle feet around to secure solid footing. Ball played slightly inside left heel. Firm grip and blade laid open.

52. SIDE VIEW, TRAP SHOT STANCE AND ADDRESS. Weight back
on heels. Arms hanging straight down and hands well in toward body.

104

53. TOP OF BACK SWING. Feet flat throughout entire swing. Glue eyes to selected spot behind ball and do not take eyes off this spot. Do not look at ball at all. Swing slightly from outside and aim a bit to left of hole.

105

54. IMPACT. Showing method of taking sand in back of ball in explosion shot. Striking spot varies with consistency of sand and distance to traverse. Resolve to go all the way through on all trap shots. Do not attempt to check club at any point in forward swing.

The Hattstrom "In-Line" Putting Technique

The Hattstrom "In-Line" Putting Technique

PUTTING IS A GAME within a game. No other phase of golf has received anywhere nearly the attention that putting has been given. Golfing minds have designed and produced countless varieties of putters, from the standard type blade down to the freak eighteen-inch long hammer-headed abortion designed for one hand use. Reams have been written about putting grips. Putting stances have also come in for much discussion. One can see almost any sort of physical contortion on the green from a stiff upright stance to the ludicrous method of putting between the legs from a backward position "because he could see a straighter line to the cup that way."

No doubt all of these ideas have merit and if any of them suits the particular player's style and he gets good results with it, then that's the technique for him. Any method that gets the ball into the hole consistently is all right. From all this variation and palaver on putting, the average golfer might deduce that putting was an extremely important branch of the game. Well, I'll go farther and say that the putter is the most inportant club in the bag. Nowhere else can you save as many strokes as you can on the green. Big tournaments are won on the greens, and not off the tees or on the fairways. Put your money on the player who's on the beam with his putter, and nine times out of ten you'll come out ahead.

Since putting is so important, let's dissect it and see what makes it tick. First we will define putting. Putting is the *stroking* of a ball and nothing else. Note that we said *stroking* and not *hitting.* One hears of stroking the shot with all the other clubs too, but in no sense has the term "stroking" as true a meaning as it has in putting. The smooth stroking of a putt has more the similarity of your hand softly stroking a silken fur. Let that thought sink so deeply into your consciousness that your sub-conscious mind will automatically transmit this thought to you everytime you hold a putter in your hands. There can never be a jabbed or stabbed putt where the slow, smooth, swinging stroke is employed.

The best way to produce smooth stroking is by the pendulum method of swinging which is easily and definitely accomplished with the *Hattstrom "IN-LINE" Technique.* In order to obtain the proper pendulum effect we must have the right tool to do it with, so we will now discuss putters. I have been a fanatical experimenter with putters, and over a golfing span of thirty years I have tried out myriad varieties of both standard and eccentric putters of every make and description. I sincerely believe that if I had kept them all I would probably have a collection worthy of museum space. All this experimentation proved one important thing. If you want to stroke a ball properly in the pendulum manner you must have a club heavy enough in the head to do it with. Weight in the head will make you swing the club and not jerk it. The blade type putter usually supplied with a regular set of clubs is generally too thin and too light in the head to be effective. The light weight head is conducive to hitting, jerking, and stabbing. A putt that is hit or jabbed may or may not stay on the line, whereas a putt stroked with a heavy club hugs it religiously. Putts that are "hit" often get a "pinched" effect on the ball which produces in the first few feet either a backspin or a skidding action before it begins to roll. This type of ball can easily veer from side to side and if struck a little too hard will slide right over the hole. It is also easily deflected by both grass and loose impediments on the green. The stroked putt with the heavy putter produces an overspin effect which makes the ball travel straight and true. The overspin putt will travel farther with less impact than any other. It will climb scuffed grass, loose impediments, and so on, and still stay in line. But best of all, the overspin putt will dive when it hits the hole even though it may have been stroked too hard. There will also be more "dying" putts made with the overspin ball. They will drop in from the "side and back doors" more often than will other ball actions.

The more or less center shafted putters are fairly well suited for pendulum swinging, but the greatest difficulty seems to be in getting one with enough of an upright lie. The general run of putters are a bit on the flat side which puts the ball too far away. The arc of the swing with flat-lie putters is such that a ball can be easily pulled or pushed out of line—especially on long putts. The upright putter swings directly in the line of the putt, and hence the direction is greatly improved. Where you cannot secure a putter with enough upright lie to it, a professional or pro shop clubmaker can bend or knock a clubhead upright if the hosel is of the malleable type.

Putters with square grips, or grips that are flat on top and round underneath, are good aids in putting since the thumbs must lie directly on top of the shaft. Some putters have pistol or polo grip ends that also help in gaining smooth control. The Hagen Gold Star, Spalding Horton Smith, MacGregor Tommy Armour Iron Master, and Wilson Mark Harris models are some of the putters with malleable necks and hosels that can easily be converted into the upright pendulum swinging type suitable to the Hattstrom *In-Line* Technique. Some of the Hillerich and Bradsby center shafted putters with square grips are also suitable.

Many golfers who have become very proficient putters with my "In-Line" method have urged me to design a special putter to fit the technique. After considerable experimentation I designed the Hattstrom *In-Line* Putter and a companion run-up club, embodying all the desirable features necessary in these clubs.

The Putting Grip

THE PUTTING GRIP is another important subject with many angles for discussion. There are several putting grips, all of which have their good points. However, since we are discussing and recommending the pendulum method of stroking a ball we will confine our remarks to the grip most suitable for its proper execution. The reverse overlapping grip is used. In this grip the putter is held by the tips of all fingers of the right hand and by tips of last three of left hand. The index finger of the left hand points straight down and overlaps the fingers of the right hand (57 and 58).

The index finger of the left hand in this position guides the club on the back swing. Thumbs must be placed directly on top of shaft. In this position the back of the left hand and the palm of the right are facing directly to the hole. One of the secrets of good putting is in the proper position of the club shaft in the hands. In the regular grip with the woods and irons the club is held diagonally across the hand and fingers with the shaft resting against the heel of the hand. In the putting grip the shaft comes up through the center of the hand, practically between the base of the thumb and the heel (55 and 56).

In the grip with the other clubs it was necessary to have a firm hold with the left hand and a lighter grip with the right. The putting grip is just the reverse. Grip with the left should be definitely on the light side and the right should be just gently firm—just enough grip to keep club from wobbling out of line. Predominance of right hand grip will be between thumb and index finger. Left hand will take club back and right hand will take charge on forward stroke. Stroke is made entirely with wrists, therefore wrists must be kept loose and flexible, simply acting as hinges.

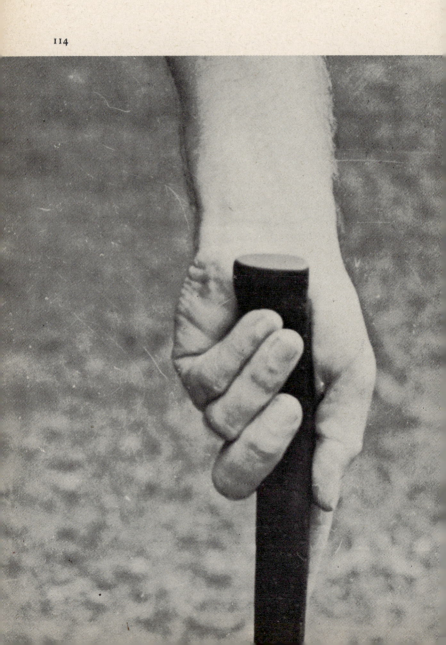

56. RIGHT HAND GRIP. This position further enhances the upright, almost vertical position of the club shaft so desirable in the true pendulum stroke.

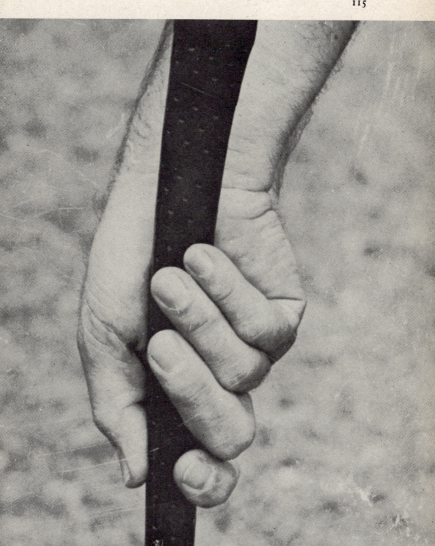

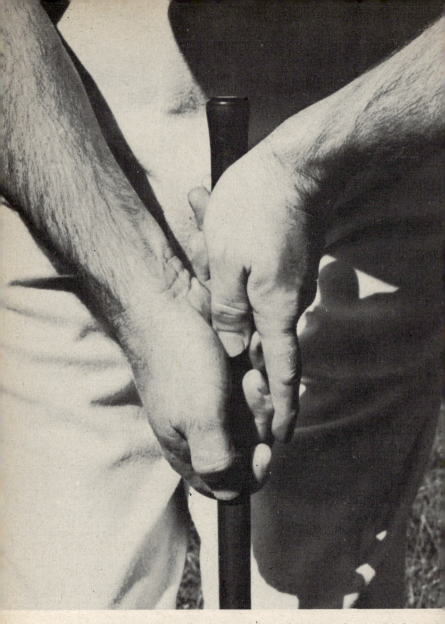

57. PUTTING GRIP. Reverse overlap with index finger of left hand overlapping fingers of right and pointing straight down. See (58) for proper right hand grip. Club is held by tips of all fingers of right hand and tips of last three of left hand. Shaft runs up through middle of hands between base of thumbs and heel. Light grip with left and gently firm with right. Both thumbs on top.

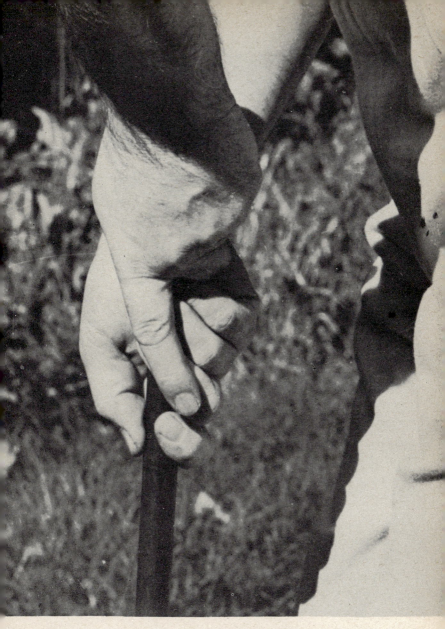

58. SIDE VIEW OF PUTTING GRIP. Showing position of left index finger which is the guiding factor in taking club back.

The Putting Stance

THE PUTTING STANCE is still another subject full of all sorts of controversial possibilities. There are as many putting stances as there are kinds of people and they will all perform after a fashion. Some golfers could probably stand on their heads and putt better than others could in the normal fashion. For the pendulum system there are only two stances that really prove satisfactory and in both the basic principle is the same. No. 1 and preferred stance: place both feet squarely at right angles to line of putt and about two to four inches apart (59). Squaring the feet this way psychologically fixes the line of putt in the mind more firmly. Also the follow through will be more readily made toward the hole. When the toes are pointed out as they are in an open stance the tendency is to pull the putt to the left of the hole. In the pendulum method we want everything to be on the square. Head, shoulders, body, hips, hands, feet, and clubhead should all be square to the line of putt.

The weight should be equally distributed between the two feet. The knees should be slightly flexed and the body bent over only enough to accommodate the length of putter, and to bring the left eye directly over the ball. The ball is played directly opposite the left toe and is placed not more than about four or five inches away from the left toe. Now here is an important item to remember. Crook the left elbow in such a way that it points directly to the hole (59 and 61). This elbow position keeps the left hand and wrist in the vertical position making a perfect swinging point for the pendulum weight. This position also prevents the right hand from pushing the club off line. The club will just naturally follow through to the hole.

59. PUTTING STANCE AND ADDRESS. Feet close together and both feet square to line of putt. Knees flexed and body bent over enough to accommodate length of putter and to get left eye directly over ball. Left elbow crooked so that it points to hole. Hands in same plane as clubhead, being neither ahead of it nor behind it. Clubface square to line. Ball played opposite left toe.

60. PUTTING STANCE AND ADDRESS, SIDE VIEW. This photograph illustrates closeness of ball to left toe, being not more than four or five inches away, which brings the eyes directly over ball from where the line of putt can easily be seen.

62. ALTERNATE PUTTING STANCE AND ADDRESS. All details the same as in (59) except feet are wider apart and weight practically all on left foot.

122

The Pendulum Stroke

EXECUTION OF PENDULUM STROKE: after the line of putt has been established, place clubhead squarely in back of ball with ball at center of club face. The club is taken back along the line of putt by the index finger of the left hand. The length of back swing is governed entirely by distance to the hole. Forward swing is made with the right hand with predominence of grip between the thumb and index finger. Let clubhead swing clear through the ball toward the hole. Do not check or stop clubhead at any point on the forward swing. Keep face of clubhead square to line of putt during entire swing backward and forward. Avoid open or closed faces. Stroke should be made very definitely on the slow and relaxed side. Never hurry a putt. Stroke should be made entirely with hands and wrists, regardless of distance to be negotiated. Do not permit arms or body to get into stroke. Ball should be struck squarely in the back. The clubhead swinging on through creates an upward drag on the ball which imparts the desirable overspin.

To those who are so nervously constructed that they find it difficult to relax sufficiently to execute a slow, deliberate stroke, the following technique is recommended. This method might be justifiably called the "make 'em or miss 'em quick" system. Place the clubhead on the green in front of the ball. Square the blade on the line of putt. Now pick up club and momentarily set clubhead down again, this time behind the ball. Immediately start the backswing, exactly as before. The secret of this system seems to be in keeping the whole action constantly on the move, avoiding hesitation anywhere in the stroke. This motion keeps the muscles and nervous system fluid and avoids jerkiness in the stroke.

63. PUTTER BACK SWING. Backswing shown here is approximate swing for a five foot putt. Length of backswing is controlled entirely by distance to go. All putts are made with the wrists only, regardless of distance to go. Note here that wrists are in control and not the arms. Club is taken back along line with left hand and guided by index finger. Keep club face square at all times. Execute stroke slowly.

64. PUTTER FORWARD SWING. Right hand takes charge on forward swing. Stroke through the ball, and finish with club face still square to line and facing hole.

65. PUTTER BACK SWING, SIDE VIEW. Club has been taken back same distance as in (63). Note that clubhead is directly in putting line.

126

66. PUTTER FORWARD SWING, SIDE VIEW. Ball has been smoothly stroked and is on way to hole. Clubhead still is in putting line with face finishing to hole.

127

Some Putting Suggestions

SOME PUTTING SUGGESTIONS: never be careless on a single putt regardless of how short it may be. Even six inch putts may be missed. Line up the putt from both sides of the hole if necessary and observe all green undulations. Survey the line to the hole, and observe whether the grain of the grass is with, against, or across the line of putt. Pick up or brush away all loose impediments in the line. Select a spot from two to four feet ahead of the ball and use this as your aiming guide. Make the ball definitely roll over this spot. Locate this spot by crouching down to the green and sighting from about five to eight feet behind the ball.

Always try to hole every putt regardless of distance. "Never up, never in" is good putting logic. Of all putts over fifteen feet, 80 per cent end up short of the hole. To combat this, imagine you are putting for a hole that is two feet beyond the actual hole on distances from ten to fifteen feet. On putts from twenty to twenty-five feet, visualize the hole as being three feet beyond, and so on for longer distances. Don't be afraid to go for the hole, for there is just as much room on the other side of the hole as there is on this side. The chances are you'll have a shorter putt coming back if you miss the first than you'd have by being short. Be Scotchly parsimonious with your putts. Dread three-putt greens like poison — simply determine not to have them. Never be satisfied with a two-putt-per-green average either. That sort of program is all right for the pros who are on the greens in regulation shots or less. The 85 or less shooter who is often short of the green and is able to run short ones in close to the pin, should not have over 32 putts to the round. Make yourself extremely putt conscious by recording your putts on each hole along with your total score on the hole. Strive constantly to better your lowest putting record even though it might be 20 putts for the round. Maybe you can lower it to 18. It's been done before. Try some serious putting practice on the putting clock. To drill yourself for extreme accuracy, stick a tee into the green and putt to it instead of to a hole. Attain such accuracy that you can hit it from all distances. Once you get used to putting at such a small object, the hole in the green will probably look like a wash tub to you in comparison. You just know that if you can hit that little tee from ten feet there won't be much difficulty in hitting a four inch hole from five feet. This creates confidence and putting is 50 per cent confidence and 50 per cent skill. If you know you're going to make the putt, you generally do. Many times you will be able to call the shot beforehand — to the amazement and bewilderment of your opponents. An egotist makes a good putter.

A Few Don'ts

A Few Don'ts

I HAVE AVOIDED placing this "don't" section in among the fore-going chapters so as not to create a maze of confusion in the golfer's mind. It is tough enough learning the elementary rudiments of golf, plus the proper procedure and execution of a golf stroke, let alone complicating matters with a lot of "don'ts."

However, once a golfer has acquired the fundamental knowledge, skill, and other essentials of a sound game, he can quickly analyze his own game as well as others. By observation he can learn much by merely watching the professionals play a shot. He has acquired enough golf knowledge to be able to imitate a swing or shot merely by having seen it played. A golfer can also learn what not to do by observing how Joe Dubb plays the game and comparing it with his own.

Let's analyze some of Joe Dubb's golfing gyrations in the following illustrations, and then make a pledge never to be guilty of any of them in the future.

67. BASEBALL GRIP. Don't use a baseball grip such as is shown above on a golf club. Former ball players are guilty of this faulty grip in their first attempts at golf. A baseball bat is gripped in the palms of the hands, which is necessary for swinging in a more or less horizontal plane. A golf club is held by the fingers and not the palms. See (1, 2, and 3) for proper grips.

68. OPPOSED GRIP. Don't use an opposed grip like this. An opposed grip prevents arms, wrists, and hands from working together as one unit. Compare this grip with proper grip shown in (1, 2, and 3).

69. BENT LEFT ARM. Don't let left arm bend in the fashion shown above. This restricts the swing arc, and causes the player to hit from top of swing directly down on the ball. There is neither power nor direction in this swing. Usually, when the left arm is bent in this manner, we find the whole left side collapsing, too, at impact. However, the left arm does not necessarily have to be as stiff and straight as a poker. Keeping it stretched out is the point.

70. LEANING OVER ON TOES. Don't have weight on toes in address or in swing. Leaning over on toes makes you fall into your shot, causing shanking and smothered shots. Keep weight back on heels throughout entire swing.

71. STIFF ARM SWING. Don't reach for the ball nor hit the ball in this stiff arm manner. Stretching in this fashion locks hand, wrists, and arms, which restricts back swing with resultant loss of power. This swing usually produces slices and bad shots off the toe of the club. Let arms and hands hang down naturally. This will keep the wrists flexible, and permit their proper hinging action. See (7, 8, 9, 29, 44, and 52) for comparison.

138

72. SWAYING. Don't sway. Moving head and hips laterally is not pivoting. A swayer can be a prolific slicer *or* hooker, depending on position of hands at impact. While it is not necessary to hold the head absolutely stone still, it is desirable to keep it from swaying. A pivot is a turn, not a sway. A swayer seldom can hit a ball from the inside out.

73. WEIGHT ON LEFT FOOT AT TOP OF SWING. Don't have your weight on the left leg at the top of your swing. This action restricts the arc of the swing on both backward and forward swings. It makes it impossible for the left side to pull the club through in the proper line. Hitting directly down from the top of the swing with the right hand is common with this swing.

74. OPENING FINGERS. Don't open fingers at top of swing. It is absolutely essential that the fingers of the left hand remain in full, firm grip throughout entire swing. Opening fingers at top of swing causes re-gripping on the down swing and a loss of control of club which destroys accuracy. Right hand will take command too soon in this case, and a hit from the top will ensue.

75. OVER SWINGING. Don't overswing. Much better results can be had from too short a swing than from too long a swing. When club shaft falls below horizontal position, as shown in above photograph, there is a tendency for the right hand to take command too early in down swing, bringing about a right hand hit from the top. The fingers of left hand also tend to open up at top in overswinging.

76. WEIGHT ON RIGHT LEG AT IMPACT. Don't hit the ball with your weight back on the right leg. This action prevents proper follow through with a resultant loss of power and direction. It usually produces a slice.

77. RESTRICTED FOLLOW THROUGH. Don't check or stop club immediately after hitting ball. This restricted follow-through is indicative of
a jerked swing. A ball on contact is carried along for a certain distance
upon the club face, depending on how well it was hit. Where the club
is swung in a smooth, sweeping manner with a full follow through, the
ball is carried on the face of the club a longer interval than in a jerky,
choppy swing, attaining better direction and distance.

78. "FIRE AND FALL BACK." Don't acquire the "step in the bucket," or "fire and fall back" technique of hitting the ball. Nothing but a consistent and errant slice can result. Don't be afraid to move your weight onto left leg on the down swing. Compare above swing finish with that of (20 and 21).

For the Advanced Golfer

To THOSE GOLFERS who have the desire to become "in-the-seventies" shooters, it is suggested that this chapter dealing with the expert strokes will be valuable.

Good average golf can be played without knowledge of these expert shots but the nearer you get to par the more necessary it is to have these shots in the bag. In almost every round of golf there are occasions calling for plays of intentional slices or hooks; with, against, and across the wind; uphill, downhill, and sidehill lies; push shots, and so on. Being able to play these shots will save many strokes for the par or near par shooter.

To the average player these shots come under the heading of trick shots. However, to the golfer who has absorbed a fair amount of golfing knowledge there is nothing intricate or difficult about them. All they require is sufficient time, patience, and practice to execute them consistently. They must be studied and played enough to be sufficiently impressed upon the memory so that one does not forget the details of the shot, nor when it is to be used. Remember, practice and more practice is required to maintain an "in-the-seventies" rating, and this doesn't mean hitting an occasional extra ball during your weekly or bi-weekly round of golf. And don't forget either, that one hour per week practice session in the sand traps. The scratch player who is always going all out for the green on his second or third shot will find himself in the traps probably more often than the 10 handicapper, and therefore has definite need for a dependable trap shot.

Playing the Wind

THE EXPERT GOLFER makes good use of the wind, and some interesting shots can be played with its aid. The most thrilling shot I have ever played was made by the aid of the wind. This occurred on the 18th hole at the Glencoe Golf Club in Glencoe, Illinois. The hole is some 560 yards long and runs due north. On this particular day a stiff north breeze was blowing dead against me. My third shot was a bad pull to the left, which placed the ball not quite hole high, and about fifty yards away from the green.

I could not play any kind of shot directly toward the green, because there was a high tree, a drinking fountain, the 10th tee benches, and an intervening trap in my line which precluded my attempting any sort of low running shot. Being too close to the tree, it was impossible to play a high niblick over it. I elected to play an intentional slice with the No. 7 mashie niblick. I faced directly north, dead against the wind, and played a crisply hit cut shot. The ball started out to go straight ahead, and at the same time gained altitude. It passed the tree on the left, and climbed to about a hundred and fifty foot height to where the cut spin began to take hold. The ball then started to curve to the right. The ball had been hit hard enough to carry it some twenty-five yards beyond the green, but now the wind took charge. When the spin had spent itself, the ball floated back south to the green. It hit the green at top center, and the ball rolled down three feet past the hole where it was an easy matter to sink the putt for a par 5. In this shot the ball traveled an arc that almost completed a semi-circle — practically a boomerang.

It would have been impossible to play such a shot unless the wind had been there as an aid, so I repeat again, that many interesting shots can be pulled off by making good use of the wind instead of fighting it.

Three types of tee shots can be used with the wind. The normal stroke can be used, of course, but to take advantage of the wind for distance, high balls played with the driver and brassie are preferable. When using the driver for this shot, tee the ball high, and play it well up off the left toe. Keep hands back of clubhead and use a long sweeping arc swing. Ball should be sweepingly struck on the upstroke. When stroked in this manner the ball remains in contact with the club face, and more overspin will be imparted. This ball will carry a long way, and will run a considerable distance when it hits the turf.

Another good shot with the wind is the one played with the brassie off the tee. A normal stance is used, with the ball in regular teeing position. The ball is hit hard with the brassie, causing it to start out low and then begin to climb. The brassie loft tends to impart a slight back spin which causes the ball to climb to a good height. When the spin has spent itself, the wind will take charge, and the ball will float with it. This shot will have a long carry, but will not run as much as the ball hit on the upstroke with the driver.

PLAYING AGAINST THE WIND disturbs more golfers than anything else. Psychologically they immediately visualize a well-hit ball rising abruptly into the wind, and going nowhere. To compensate, they will try to hit the ball harder. Naturally, pressing results. Pressing for distance against the wind will never get a golfer anywhere. There is just one simple rule to remember in playing against the wind — hit the ball as easily and lazily as you can! When a ball is stroked easily, it is carried along on the face of the club for a longer period than when it is hit hard. This gives the club face a chance to roll on the ball and impart an overspin. An overspin ball will bore into the wind instead of rising, as in the case of backspin.

Playing approaches to the green into the wind presents no

unusual difficulty. Simply use the next longest club and play for the top of the flag, letting the wind act as a brake.

When wind is from the right, play an intentional hook along the right edge of the fairway. If wind is from the left, play an intentional slice along the left side of the fairway. Making use of the wind in this manner adds to the distance. When playing an iron approach to the green under cross winds, the reverse technique should be used. With wind from the right, play the approach with a slight slice cut on the ball, which will hold the ball up into the wind and drop it dead on the green. If the wind is from the left, play a slight hook shot for the same effect.

THE PUSH SHOT is one of the finest shots in golf, but it is rather difficult to execute. This shot is usually played with a long iron, and is used where a long, low shot is required. It is a great shot against the wind. Since wind near the ground is never as strong as aloft, the push shot is not therefore affected by it, due to its low trajectory. It is also a good shot when playing for a long, low shot under trees, and so on. It has a peculiar characteristic in that the ball seems to travel as fast as a bullet, and yet, despite its low trajectory, it has very little run at the finish.

A square stance is used with the weight retained on the left foot throughout the entire swing. The ball is played in center, with the hands well ahead of clubhead. Club face is kept square to ball, which makes a still straighter face. A No. 2 iron in this position actually becomes a No. 1 iron. This slightly hooded effect of the club face helps in pinching the ball between the blade and the ground, and also in keeping the ball low. The wrists and arms are held taut, since this is more of a stabbing or pushing stroke. The head is held very steady, and very little pivot is made. The swing is executed from a half shot position, and the ball is struck first in such a manner that it is pushed or squeezed against the turf at impact. Only a slight divot is taken after the ball. At the point of impact, the entire weight should be on the left foot, and the body should have a definite lean toward the objective. The push shot requires plenty of practice to perfect, but it is well worth the effort. It is one shot that'll really pay off when you need it.

80. PUSH SHOT IMPACT. This photograph depicts the proper left side action at impact of push shot. Left hip is decidedly thrust out toward objective with the hands coming in well ahead of clubhead. In this manner the ball is more or less "pushed" against the turf.

The Intentional Slice

THE INTENTIONAL SLICE is a grand shot to call upon on occasions where a left to right shot is needed to go around some object in the line; or when playing a narrow fairway where it might be safer to play along the left side with the intention of having the ball end up in the middle. Many golfers tighten up when called upon to play a narrow fairway, and in trying to hit a straight ball down the center invariably hook or slice into trouble. Since it is easier to play a slice than a hook, it is therefore preferable to play an intentional slice along the left side rather than playing a hook along the right side, unless, of course, you have a strong cross wind from the right, which then would call for a hook along the right side.

81. INTENTIONAL SLICE STANCE AND ADDRESS. Use an open stance for the intentional slice. The left foot should be drawn back four or five inches from right foot line. The left toe is turned out, the right foot square. Since pivot should be restricted in a slice shot, placing the right foot square will help to prevent getting around too far. The ball is played well forward, and hands are slightly behind clubhead. The right hand is placed a bit more on top, with V pointing up the center of body.

82. INTENTIONAL SLICE SWING. The club is taken back on the outside with left hand. Take club up to a higher than normal position at top. Swing through from outside and finish with clubhead low. Be sure to aim to left of desired objective. See (25) for position of shaft at top of swing for slice.

83. INTENTIONAL HOOK STANCE AND ADDRESS. The intentional hook is played practically in reverse to the slice. The hook is sometimes called a draw or pull shot. A closed stance is used with the right foot drawn back four or five inches. The right toe is pointed out to permit a freer turn and the left foot is square. The ball is played about center, and hands are slightly ahead of clubhead. The right hand is placed more to right, with V pointing to outside edge of right shoulder.

84. FINISH OF INTENTIONAL HOOK SWING. The swing for an intentional hook is the exact reverse of the slicing method. The club is taken back on inside with left hand and with a full body turn. The club need not have the high address at top of the swing, but club shaft must be in a 1:30 to 7:30 across-the-line-of-flight position. See (22 and 23) for simulated position. Swing down and through from inside and finish high. Letting the hands roll over at impact increases the hook spin on ball. The aim should be to the right of objective.

85. DOWNHILL LIE, STANCE AND ADDRESS. Tactics on downhill lies are the reverse of those on uphill. Use open stance with left foot drawn back, and weight on left foot. Ball is played opposite left heel. The swing is nearly the same as for an intentional slice — being slightly from the outside. Be sure to aim to left of objective to allow for natural slice from this lie. Use a higher lofted club such as a No. 3 or 4 wood to gain height in carry.

86. SIDEHILL LIE WHEN STANDING BELOW BALL. To play a sidehill hanging lie when standing below the ball, use a closed stance with right foot drawn back. Play ball from center position. Take a shorter grip on club, and swing in normal manner. Aim to right of objective as hooks are naturals from these lies.

87. SIDEHILL LIE, STANDING ABOVE BALL. The method of playing this lie is a reverse of the technique used for standing below the ball. Use open stance with left foot drawn back. Play ball opposite left heel. Take a longer grip on club, and swing in normal fashion. Aim to left of objective, as slices are natural results when playing from this type of lie.